Soul Tribe:

Navigating the Spiritual War

LAURA VAN TYNE

ISBN: 9798521290109

DEDICATION

There is a battle between forces of darkness and light for control of this planet and its inhabitants. This book is dedicated to those who seek the light and the truth so we may all regain our soul sovereignty and exist in love and light.

CONTENTS

ACKNOWLEDGMENTS

I am blessed to have so many wonderful and supportive people in my life.

To my family, ours has not been an easy journey as we learned to navigate the unseen world together. My love for you is eternal. I could not imagine doing this without you.

To my dear friend, CS, who literally pulled me up many lifetimes ago. There are no words to describe our friendship other than "comma quote".

To Caryn who has been my sounding board, I am very grateful to you and our conversations.

To, whom I fondly call, "The ECETI Ladies". A group of women I met at an out of state conference, only to learn they lived right down the road from me. Cindy, Gina, Lan, Therese, Lois, and Robin thank you for being there.

To my manager, Judi, who knows exactly how and how far to push me. I wouldn't be able to help as many people as I do without your guidance.

Finally, to my editor Michelle. You are one of those kind and rare souls that seems to know exactly what is needed.

Thank you for your unconditional love and support. You all make the world a better place. Love, Laura

The Spiritual War

We have been in a spiritual war for many millennia. It has shown up with many different faces throughout the history of the planet. In order for this planet to be settled in light and life, for this planet and its inhabitants to evolve, we need to clean up the dark elements. These negative entities have been puppeting us since before the Spanish Inquisition, World War I and II, and into the present-day Clown Show and Info Wars. The prize is the planet and its inhabitants.

We are not alone. We are spiritual beings far before we were ever human beings. The spiritual being aspect of us is our soul. Our physical bodies are merely temporary as they house the soul.

When we incarnate here, we arrive with a plan and a spiritual team, or Soul Tribe, in place. They watch over us. They guide us. No two spiritual teams are exactly alike.

We all have a Soul Tribe, whether we are aware of it or not. Our soul's tribe, those beings and entities from other realms and dimensions are here to assist us on our mortal journey. It's important to understand and recognize that our Soul Tribe will change as we change.

However, here's where it gets a bit tricky. Not all Soul Tribes pitch for the same team. In other words, they are not all good guys. In fact, the bad guys try to infiltrate our Soul Tribe all the time. This is why it's important to know and understand how your Soul Tribe operates.

Our Soul Tribes are karmically earned. The spiritual team we start out with at birth changes as we go through mortal life. The key is simple. It's about frequency. The more we learn, study and apply wisdom, the more we are able to raise our frequency. The higher we can raise our frequency, the more we connect to God, the Divine, Source, Creator, or whatever term you use. The deeper our connection is to our Soul Tribe, the more closely we can be to Source.

Have you ever had a feeling that something was about to happen, and it did? Chances are that was your Soul Tribe warning you or showing you a particular path to follow. Have you ever seen a light figure out of the corner of your eye? Chances are that was a member or two of your Soul Tribe. Many times, I can feel my Soul Tribe touch me. It feels like light bubbles on my left arm. That's how I know it is them and that they are around me. These tiny bubbles have a distinct frequency or familiarity with them. There have been other times when I would feel a different type of touch on my arm, and I knew it wasn't my Soul Tribe. More on that later.

With intention and knowledge, we can actually improve the quality and quantity of our Soul Tribe so best help us in this lifetime, our life between lifetimes and even our future lives. The more we can work to enhance the quality of our Soul Tribe, the healthier our soul becomes. Our soul is the only aspect that is ever truly ours. Our souls are sovereign, or at least they are supposed to be.

Today we need to do things differently, and that is to understand we all have a spiritual team, a Soul Tribe. We all have the power and access to create a powerful Soul Tribe with intention and discernment. Our soul is the only element that we will ever truly own.

It's up to us to make sure our soul is sovereign and in good health. This book addresses factors that affect all of us, all of our souls. It will also show you what you can do to ensure you have the best possible Soul Tribe possible. It is time we realize our soul sovereignty and fight back in the spiritual war that has been ever present.

Understanding Dimensions

We need to truly understand how the different dimensions work and operate in order to fully grasp how this spiritual war works. It is imperative to know that while we are currently residing in the third dimension, there are other dimensions that have a direct impact and influence our daily lives. In order to build the best Soul Tribe, or spiritual team for our soul, we need a basic understanding of the beings and entities and where they reside.

We are living in the third dimension. This dimension requires time, space and gravity. These three ingredients are what gives us our physical, mortal world. This is the dimension in which we are currently living. This is our physical, mortal world. This is our tangible world where we use our five senses of sight, hearing, touch, smell and taste. The physical body we are born with merely serves as a cloak for what lies beneath -- our personality, our intuition, and the energetic love that pulses in and out of our hearts.

This is the dimension into which our souls incarnate and reincarnate. We return here within our soul or family groups for the lessons and experiences we need on our karmic path for our soul's evolution (hopefully). It's important to realize that our souls are eternal, and our physical bodies are only used for this specific incarnation. However, our physical bodies that we incarnate into are based on our karma and our soul's specific needs for those lessons, experiences, soul purposes, and possibly a soul mission.

It doesn't mean that someone who gets cancer or has a life changing accident *deserved* that. It *might* be that those around that person need to have the experiences of caring for someone else and learning greater depths of compassion and love. The same is true for a child born with some type of disability or anomaly. It's a karmic opportunity which offers us many rich experiences. This world is where each of us has chosen to incarnate (or reincarnate) for the experiences and lessons our souls need on our karmic path. Our souls are eternal, but our physical bodies are only used for this current incarnation.

How does free will fit in? Mortal man has been gifted free will. This is an important concept to understand as we move forward. Free will means we have the ability to make choices. Every decision we make earns us karma. Karma in its most basic form is simply action and reaction. It's also called the law of consequences. You get angry and kick something hard and you end up causing yourself pain and possibly breaking something.

Karma is not fatalistic or predetermined. Karma is our ability to create and change our circumstances based on actions and environments that we experience. Karma spans our soul's entire existence. Karma may not be satisfied in one single lifetime. Karma is not emotional nor judgmental. It is not vengeful. Karma is simply balance.

It's important to understand this a bit as we talk about other dimensions. When we incarnate into physical bodies and live a mortal life, we have the ability to make choices. Every choice we make earns us karma.

The fourth dimension was originally meant to be a step-up transformer from the mortal realm to the higher realms, so that we can go Home. The original intention of this dimension was to be kind of like the way station when we leave our physical bodies. If you think about it, our physical bodies are really like rental units. When we die and move on, we don't take them with us.

Some groups call this dimension purgatory, the hells, limbo, the lower astral. It can go by many names. But here is what it really is:

When it's our time to 'go' and we leave our physical body, the energy that animated that body, our soul, has to go somewhere. The first law of thermodynamics states that energy is neither created nor destroyed. It can, however, be transformed or transferred from one form to another. Think of how water works. The energy that is water, can become a solid, liquid or a gas. It is still H2O. The concept is the same, but the widget is different. This is true for our souls, as well.

The energy that animates our physical body has to go somewhere when we die, and that is the fourth dimension. The trick is not to stay there. Ideally, when we die, we go to the fourth dimension, see the light and cross over into the next dimension.

The fourth dimension, however, has become contaminated with dark entities who fell from the light of God. As was stated earlier, these dark entities that fell from the higher realms had to go somewhere, but where? These dark entities realized they could set up shop in the fourth dimension. This was a brilliant move on their part. Why? Because the mortals (humans) are of the light, they are created from Source, and they have to pass through the fourth dimension to go Home. This is where the dark forces have been residing for many millennia. They have been hiding in plain sight. We need to understand that this was not the original purpose of this dimension. Ghost energies, or soul energies, are soul food for these dark entities. The dark ones will capture soul energies and use them for their energetic gains. When this happens, the soul becomes diminished and more and more broken down.

The concept of ghosts, angels, and demons exist in every location, every culture throughout the history of this planet. If they didn't exist, then why would this be the case? In literature and in the arts, for example, we often hear of angels and demons. In the Renaissance, period they are depicted throughout Europe in the forms of literature, paintings, and even in philosophies, spanning from the 14th to the 17th century AD.

The Bhagavad Gita is theorized to have been written somewhere around the 5th to the 3rd century, BC. Chapter 16 of this holy text includes details about the spiritual war at hand, the negative and the benevolent spirits who exist in the non-material world, and how they impact our daily lives. These are just two of the many examples that can be found in different eras and locations.

Many people have had paranormal experiences. All over the globe there are purported places that are haunted where 'unexplained' events happen. It's in those moments that the fourth dimension collides into the third dimension. The fourth dimension impacts our mortal world all the time, whether we are aware of it or not. Whether we believe in it or not.

What is a ghost? A ghost is a human who has died, left their physical body and got stuck in the fourth dimension—literally stuck between Heaven and Earth. We have been programmed to believe otherwise. We say, "They deserve to rot in hell," or "It's their choice to not cross over," or "They have unfinished business." Let me tell you, when a person dies and leaves their body, all of their mortal business is finished. It's not like they can go to work and collect a paycheck or sit down and eat a meal with the family. There is no such thing as unfinished business. Every single soul needs to cross over no matter how they lived or died.

Why and how does a soul become a ghost? The short and simple answer is that the soul becomes trapped between Heaven and Earth, and there are many reasons why this can happen. Sometimes the soul doesn't know they have died. Perhaps they feel guilty or not worthy. Maybe they committed suicide and their grief and despair was so great they couldn't see the light that came for them. Or perhaps the Luciferic, or Dark Forces created a net to trap them so that they could not cross over.

Furthermore, it is imperative to understand that even the evilest of humans needs to cross over into the Heavens. Why? So that they don't torment the living. I had a client who was raped by a neighbor when she was a child. She came to me as an adult because she felt something was haunting her and she didn't know what it was. She was not able to sleep. When she actually did sleep, she would wake up with strange bruises on her thighs and bite marks all over her body. As I worked with her, we found that the haunting was the rapist who had died in prison, and my client did not know he had died. We crossed him over and her issues stopped. The ghost rapist became infatuated with harming her. He felt that he owned her soul, and he was determined to take it back.

We all have the ability and power to help the dead cross over, so they do not become stuck in the fourth dimension. If you find you have a ghost or many ghosts with you, use the Crossing Over Souls Prayer at the end of this book to help them cross over. It is important to never assume that a loved one has crossed over when they died.

When we help a soul to cross over, we are

changing their soul health and soul path for the better for eternity. When a soul languishes in the fourth dimension, they are chronically cold, hungry, and are often harassed by dark entities in the fourth dimension. When this happens, their soul energy (their essence) starts to degrade, and they become weaker and more and more broken.

We have been programmed to believe that if we can talk to the dead, then they are fine. The harsh truth is that when our mortal time here is done on this planet, karmically our soul needs to return Home for healing, restoration, and guidance on the life just lived. That soul's karmic time here is done for now. These elements will never happen in the fourth dimension. It is also important to note that when we die, we are not supposed to interfere with the living mortals in the third dimension. Every single person who dies needs to be crossed over. When we do this, the dark entities that reside in the fourth dimension no longer have access to their soul.

It's time we take a hard look at what happens

in the fourth dimension. It is my belief that this dimension has a larger impact on our souls than most people realize. This dimension contains more than just ghosts. It is full of unseen negative energies and entities that feast on these souls.

If you can see or sense beings in other dimensions, it is very important to remember to use absolute discernment and caution. I cannot stress enough <u>NOT</u> to blindly trust the energy or image that you see. The beings in the fourth dimension are very slick, and can fool you very easily, as they can scan your internal self and your thoughts. This concept also holds true in our physical, third dimensional world, where often what we see, whom we trust, or sense, can suddenly change and alter its appearance. Or where a temporal influence may be targeting you or someone else.

In our third dimensional, mortal world we have a hierarchy and a political structure. The fourth dimension is no different. There are many types of nefarious beings and entities that reside there, some have more influence than others and they all have bosses.

Next, we need a clear understanding of the various types of hauntings that can happen when the third and fourth dimensions collide.

Fourth Dimensional Residents

There are many different types of entities that reside in the fourth dimension. All entities that reside in this dimension are lower frequency beings. Getting an understanding of who and what resides there, gives us our power back. When we understand how this dimension truly impacts us all in our mortal lives, we have the opportunity to gain the knowledge needed to ensure sovereignty for our souls.

Ghostly souls reside in the fourth dimension. A ghost is simply a former human who died and is stuck between dimensions—between Heaven and Earth. Ghosts are not the only beings who reside in this dimension. This is where the problem lies when it comes to learning about and developing our Soul Tribe. These dark entities would love to infiltrate your Soul Tribe. This problem greatly affects the living in many ways. If ghosts can interfere with us, then so can these other beings. It's simply a logic trail. This is a large part of the problem and it's happening on a global scale. We keep hearing the words 'cabal' and 'satanism' and we are hearing of the unspeakable when it comes to pedophilia rings. We wonder what makes a living person do the unspeakable. But somewhere along the way a variety of dark entities took up residence and took over the fourth dimension.

Hat Man or Man with a Hat: He is called this because he appears to be wearing a fedora style hat. You can see pictures of him throughout the history of the planet and in many locations. This entity is more of an observer and a reporter. Years ago, we had one existing in our house and it took up residence in my daughter's bedroom. It was there 24/7. It never talked, never moved. The evil that it exuded was terrifying. I don't know his purpose other than to observe and collect data. To this day, I can't stand the sight of a fedora.

Shape shifters: These entities love to disguise themselves as other beings, perhaps Jesus, your grandma, a celebrity, or anything in between. These beings can read our minds and influence us with dark thoughts. These thoughts are not yours and they are imparted or implanted within your soul. It is a form of entity attachment. In the tools section, there are strategies to break free from them. Their goal is to use low frequency thoughts and emotions so that they can feed off of us.

There is a documentary Beware of Angels. It talks about a Sunday school group that started channeling angels. This group let their egos get in the way and some bad things happened. If you can see or sense beings in other dimensions, it is really important to not blindly trust who or what you are communicating with is who or what they say they are. This concept also holds true in our physical, third dimensional world. How many times have we read that some beloved priest, soccer coach or whoever ended up being a pedophile? The same thing can happen in the fourth dimension.

I remember a friend of mine whose mother died, and I helped her to cross her mother over. My friend had a teenage daughter who was devastated by the loss of her grandma and this teenager was pretty psychic. She had a friend who told her she could summon grandma with a Ouija board. And that is what they did- or that is what they thought they did. My friend's daughter was so excited to talk to her 'crossed over' grandma that she told her mom and me what she did. I asked her to call in her grandma. And she was so proud and excited to do this. Once 'Grandma' was summoned, I visualized myself pouring salt all over 'grandma' and she shape shifted into a nasty wraith creature with yellow and red eyes. This dark entity's goal was to work its way into the young girl's Soul Tribe. I immediately requested my Soul Tribe to remove this entity and to take it to the appropriate realm so it would no longer impact the earth and those who are living on the earth.

Black magicians: These guys are a dime a dozen. They are power hungry. They are also extremely fragile. There is a hierarchy with them as well. Politics exist in all dimensions. These guys need a food source, and the easiest food source is soul food. They will attach themselves to ghosts and use their energy. When we cross over the dead, we rob them, and the other fourth dimensional beings, of a food supply and they simply starve and become weaker and weaker.

Lower Realm Entities: Have you ever seen the end of the movie Ghost? In the last scene, when the bad guy died, these things come out of the ground to take him. These are little harasser beings, and they affect the living all the time. They thrive off of negative emotional states and behaviors. Many times, we see them out of the corner of our eye and we kind of brush it off as though it was nothing. They tend to be the low man in the fourth dimensional totem pole, so to speak, and they do the bidding for other dark entities, more senior dark entities.

Knowledge is power. Knowing and understanding that these entities exist, and where they exist, takes away a large part of the power they may have over the living. It gives us the information that we need so we can start learning how they operate, and how to ensure they don't infiltrate our Soul Tribe.

The fourth dimension impacts our third dimension in many different ways. Throughout my years of working with clients I have seen many examples of how these two dimensions collide and interact with one another. Some living people are more susceptible to the energies than others, but it still has the same impact on the planet.

Reptilians and Other Low Frequency Beings: Reptilians are a type of Luciferian entity that seems to be gaining traction and notoriety in many parts of the world. They are not new to this planet. They have been here for a very long time. They have done a fabulous job concealing themselves from the mortals until recently. What has changed is their political structure. They used to have many, many types of beings and entities doing their bidding for them. Now, with the advent of knowledgeable lightworkers, many of these dark pawns have been removed from the scene, leaving the reptilians exposed and having to do their own dirty work.

When we know and understand these entities exist, it takes away their power. These entities do not have physical bodies. This is an important fact to understand. Because they do not have physical bodies, they are weak. The main tool they have used against us for millennia, is the simple fact that most living humans can't see or sense them. Just because we can't see them, doesn't mean they aren't there. Think about bacteria and viruses for a moment. We didn't believe those existed until the invention of the microscope. Once we 'learned' how to see them, we began to take our power back from the viruses and bacteria. We have come up with strategies to defeat the unseen viruses and bacteria. The same can be said for these dark entities.

Knowledge is power. This means we have the power to block, shield, and most importantly, properly remove these dark entities and send them to the appropriate realm where the higher-level beings can take charge of them.

Types of Hauntings

The Dead Haunting the Living: When a person dies, and their soul energy languishes in the fourth dimension they will impact the living. Many times, they are looking for a living person who has a bright light that they can see. Or they latch onto a living loved one in fear of not knowing what to do next. It is really a crime that as a human race, we never discuss what our soul should do upon death. Oftentimes when a person dies, the community gathers around and supports the living loved ones in their time of grief. We then say something like, "They were a good soul." Hello! They still are a good soul and that soul needs help in crossing over.

The Dead Haunting the Dead: I see this often when I am crossing over souls that have died in battle. These characters keep playing out and reliving their moments of death over and over, as if they are stuck in a never-ending loop.

The Living Haunting the Dead: There are times when the grief of a loved one is so great, that they form attachment cords to their deceased loved one and they cannot cross over. This can be common when a child dies. The death of a child is not perceived as the natural order of things. The parents' grief is so strong that they consciously, or unconsciously, don't let their child go, and the attachment is so strong that the child's soul energy gets stuck in the fourth dimension. And, oftentimes the child's soul energy is looking for an "adult" in charge as they exit their physical body.

The Living Haunting the Living: It is worth taking a moment to mention that even a living person can haunt another living person, even though they both reside in the third dimension. We often hear about someone giving someone else the "evil eye".

What is that? That is a form of negative energy that is sent from one living person to another. A classic example is the empath/narcissist relationship. The empath acts as an energetic sponge. The narcissist desires and seeks out that empath energy. The empath is often left feeling fatigued and abused. The narcissist uses the empath energy to sustain themselves.

There are also some people who can astral travel. This means they leave their bodies, usually at night, and will travel to another location. I had this experience from a woman who lived on the other side of the country. She was jealous of a relationship I had with a mutual friend. It took me a long time to figure out what was happening—why and who was causing me harm. Once I figured it out, I was able to stop it.

Dark Entities Haunting the Dead: Those Luciferic forces that reside in the fourth dimension have access to all soul energies that do not cross over. Throughout the years, I have seen the myriad of ways they torture and torment these souls. Most soul energies are captured so that these dark ones can drain them of their energy. This is a unique form of torture that will degrade and diminish the soul energy. There is no chance of healing and soul restoration from this realm. To make matters even more complicated, these souls often get reincarnated to the third dimension from here. This means that when that baby is born, it arrives at a deficit. This baby may grow into a child who harms animals or worse. It begs the question, "Is this where serial killers come from?" As mentioned earlier, it is critical for all souls to cross over to the higher realms upon mortal death.

I had a client who called me because her college-aged daughter came home from school and told her mom that she kept hearing thoughts in her head to harm her sister. She was afraid she would follow though because the thoughts were so commanding. I remote viewed the home and I found that this young woman had three ghostly entities with her, and *with them* was a black magician teaching these ghosts how to do harm. He was training these ghosts to become black magicians. I properly removed them all and the mom reported to me that all the voices in her daughter's head were now gone, and she didn't have any violent feelings or tendencies towards her sister. She is fine to this day.

Dark Entities Haunting the Living: Dark entities will also haunt the living. They can have the ability to put negative and harmful thoughts in people's heads, create depression within a person, and inhabit a living person's body. When we have a strong Soul Tribe, we have the strength and stamina to thwart these nefarious beings. This will be explained more in depth later.

Since these beings and entities from the fourth dimension negatively impact our third dimensional lives, we have spiritual jurisdiction to properly remove them and to hand them off to the beings that reside in the higher realms.

These dark entities have imparted false knowledge in many of us. One misnomer is sage. There are millions of people out there who use sage to attempt to remove all sorts of beings and energies. Sage is simply a crispy leave from a shrub. It doesn't have the spiritual horsepower to remove these things. Sage is good for sausages and ceremonies, though. If you are trying to clear your space, use Frankincense, or another high frequency resin. Think about this: What were the 3 gifts the Magi gave to the Christ child? Gold, Frankincense and Myrrh. Gold makes sense, right? So why was the Christ child gifted tree sap? Because those resins are very high frequency, and he needed all the assistance he could get.

There are many psychics, shaman and other spiritual practitioners who can see and sense these entities and remove them, by casting them away, binding them or burying them into the earth. This is not good for us or the earth. These beings are all low frequency, and when we cast off, bind, or bury them, the planet earth takes the hit. Think of it this way, if you have an infection, you will clean your wound and dress it properly. You don't wrap it up and hope the infection goes away.

Doctors scrub up between patients, so they don't cross contaminate.

When it comes to ghosts, psychics or ghost hunters who banish or cast them away, send them somewhere? But where? We may never know, but I will guarantee you they will become someone else's problem. These souls are looking for a way out of their personal hell. To banish or cast them away is simply cruel.

What Is a Soul Tribe?

Your Soul Tribe is your spiritual support team. It consists of your spirit guides and other interdimensional beings. When we incarnate here on earth, we are never alone. We arrive with our spiritual team, our soul's tribe. These spiritual beings are here to assist and guide us as we embark on our earthly journey. Our soul's tribe is earned based on the soul's history, support system, soul's purpose or sometimes even a life mission. Ideally, Divine beings come from the higher realms, from Source.

There are many types of divine beings and

entities that help us while we are living a mortal life. No two Soul Tribes are exactly alike because every soul is unique and has a different karmic path. Having a solid Soul Tribe will enhance your soul's health and well-being. We hear discussions about our physical, mental, emotional, and even our financial health. In fact, I even get emails on the health of my car. When was the last time you had a discussion about your soul's health?

Our soul's tribe helps you throughout your lifetimes and the timespan between your reincarnated lives. Tribe members may even change over time, based on your needs, actions, and most importantly, spiritual service. When we are in service to others, and that service is balanced, we begin to raise our frequency. When this happens, your Soul Tribe begins to shift to raise your frequency. You may even find that your Soul Tribe will grow and change as you evolve.

We need to remember that we are here for the experiences and lessons our souls need on our karmic paths. Our Soul Tribe knows this, and they are committed to helping us as best they can, within the confines of spiritual law. Spiritual law and karma are always operative. Spiritual laws are the laws that govern our universe and they do not change, are ever present, and constant. They aren't much different than the laws created in our physical world. The word spiritual consists of two concepts: (1) Consisting of spirit, having a spiritual being, and (2) Pertaining to the higher realms. All higher realm beings must abide by spiritual law. The higher realm beings can assist us, but only when we ask them. They cannot interfere with our free will or the free will of another.

A significant aspect of spiritual law is the concept of karma. We all incur karma, and karma is not a four-letter word. In fact, if you look closely, it's actually a five-letter word. Karma is not a negative or punitive concept. We earn karma in each of our lifetimes, and even between lifetimes. We are spiritual beings before we were ever housed inside a human body. Karma is always operative. It is simply action and reaction at its most basic level. If anyone tells you they are exempt from karma, they do not understand how karma works. Karma spans all of our lifetimes, it spans our soul's existence.

We all have free will–the ability to make decisions and choices based on our surroundings. It is also important to understand that each of our free will actions carries with it a karmic ripple effect. Our actions and reactions echo out to others all the time. Imagine you are standing in front of a still pond or a body of water. Then you pick up a handful of rocks that vary in size. What happens when you throw them all into the water? Each rock, pebble, and stone create a wave or ripple as it hits the water. Each ripple will bump into another ripple. They affect one another. Some ripples are large, some are small. But they all have an impact.

An example of a possible karmic ripple effect: If your boss is having a bad day and takes it out on his employees. Everyone gets the brunt of the boss' negative actions or comments. Then one of those employees goes home that night and carries that negative energy home and becomes argumentative and abusive to his family. That is a karmic ripple effect. One person's bad day (the boss) has impacted his entire staff, and that one or more staff member carried that toxic energy home to his family and yelled at his children—or worse. This scenario is a classic example of how our Soul Tribe can help us—if we ask. The employee can simply state the request, and it can be done mentally, "I am requesting help from my Soul Tribe to shield me from the negative energies, words, or actions of my toxic boss." Or "I am requesting insight and wisdom into how best to handle my boss today."

It is important to understand that while our Soul Tribe is here to help us, they cannot interfere with our free will. Why? Because they are here to guide and assist us. We incarnate here for the experiences and lessons our souls need and there is nothing wrong with asking for help. They can only assist us when asked otherwise they are violating our free will. This is critical to understand. The more we ask our tribe for help and guidance, the stronger our connection is to them. Communication is key. Have you ever been in a relationship with another person and for one reason or another you stop communicating with that person? Perhaps you both get really busy in your jobs, or one of you is constantly travelling. When this happens, the communications tend to break down and you may find yourself in an argument with that person or you feel a disconnect from them. The same can be said for our relationship with our Soul Tribe.

Oftentimes people will say they 'don't want to impose' on their angels, their spirit guide or any other part of their Soul Tribe. This is often because many of us have been programmed from childhood to think that what we want or need help with isn't important enough to warrant the request of these divine beings. This is false information. It creates a disconnect with our Soul Tribe and Source. It makes us feel not worthy, not important enough, as if our problems are insignificant. Nothing could be further from the truth.

Our Soul Tribe also earns karma when you give them the opportunities to help you. This helps them on their souls' evolution. Do not save up your brownie points to get the help, guidance and wisdom you seek, even for what you may think is mundane. You are only hurting yourself, and at the same time you benched your Soul Tribe. Not cool.

Our Soul Tribes are karmically earned. We earn the members who are on our Soul Tribe. We earn them based on our experiences, ability to learn lessons, our spiritual service and responsibility. Our Soul Tribe follows with us throughout our lifetimes. I know this because of the many clients I have worked with under hypnosis and their guides come in to talk with me and the client. These sessions are recorded for the client so the client can hear what is said. It is a very powerful form of healing. The higher realm beings have told me that they are assigned to people because of the living person's frequency, lessons they are here to learn and the experiences they seek. It almost feels like a giant math equation.

Another critical aspect to know about your Soul Tribe is that the team members can, and do, change based on your actions, frequencies, and experiences. Ideally, your Soul Tribe will evolve as you evolve to higher and higher frequencies. Living a life of spiritual service, learning humility, and helping to make the world a better place, will create a very strong Soul Tribe for you.

It is also possible for a person's Soul Tribe to de-evolve. Those who perpetuate violence, cause harm emotionally, and are not of spiritual service, may find their Soul Tribe de-evolving. It is a frequency issue.

Building Your Soul Tribe

With intention, we can consciously build and create our Soul Tribe. Why is this important? It is important because your soul is you. You are your soul. Your soul is the only thing that you will ever truly own. Don't you deserve the best? What are the elements to creating your Soul Tribe?

As we discussed earlier, mortal man has been gifted free will. However, with the interferences from the fourth dimension, many times our free will may actually be mitigated free will. Or what we think is free will is based on decisions we make from uninformed consent. This can happen when we have only a part of the story.

Spiritual service is another component that will help us to build our Soul Tribe. Why? Because when we are in service to others, we are working towards love, compassion and unity. Spiritual service manifests in many ways. Assisting an elderly man across the street, picking up garbage along the beach, volunteering at an animal shelter, using your prayers and mediations to help heal the world, crossing over the dead. These are all forms of spiritual service, they all earn us positive karma, and we utilize our free will to be of service to others.

Frequency is also a key element when it comes to building our Soul Tribe. The higher we can raise our frequency, or vibration, the closer and better we can connect to the higher realms. The key is to understand that we want to raise our frequency so that we have a solid baseline. When something happens to us, such as a divorce or death, our frequency will go down, but if we have a strong baseline, we don't fall as hard.

There are many ways we can learn to raise our frequency. The key is consistency. There are all types of high frequency music on the internet. If you play 528Hz music from your phone or computer at a low level, those frequencies will continue to emit and clean and clear the objects in your home. Words and thoughts are also powerful. Dr. Emoto studied the effects of words on the crystalline structures of water. In my home I wrote high frequency words on my water heater and other pipes—love, health, compassion, and hope. Being out in nature will also help to raise your frequency. When we are outside in nature, we are surrounded by negative ions (which is a good thing) and nature connects us to Source.

These are just a few things we can do with intention to build our Soul Tribe. Isn't your soul worth it?

Communicating with Your Soul Tribe

We all have access to our soul's tribe.
Communication is critical. Learning to
communicate with your Soul Tribe is critical
to your soul's growth and strength. It's more
important now than ever with intention and
discernment, to work on creating the best
Soul Tribe for you.

 We have spent millennia being disconnected
from higher dimensional frequencies. As we
learn to reconnect, we begin to reawaken and
reactivate our spiritual DNA. Our mortal
DNA is what makes us unique, it determines

our eye color, height, and the third dimensional aspects of our incarnation. Our spiritual DNA also makes us unique, and it comes from our soul and our Akashic Records.

Our Akashic Records are the records of what has happened, what is happening, and the possibilities of what will happen. It is like a giant data base. Since these records reside in a higher dimension, they are not bound by the rules of time. It is rumored that one can have access to these files. The interesting part is that everything has its own Akashic Record, including your soul. This is the blueprint to your soul. They are the records of your soul's history, present time and future possibilities.

Our spiritual DNA helps to heal and restore us to our original divine blueprint as designed by Source. Like our physical DNA, our spiritual DNA unites us as a family based on our frequency or resonance. It is human nature to be attracted to those with whom we share common goals and characteristics. The same can be said for our spiritual DNA–we resonate with those that have a similar vibration.

When learning to intentionally communicate with your Soul Tribe, mediation and prayer are critical because both connect us to our Source. Prayer is talking to your Soul Tribe, Source, Creator and mediation is listening to them. We all have the ability to do this, but we also need to practice developing these skills. This can be referred to as spiritual practices. Doctors and lawyers have practices, right? Our sovereign right as a soul is to develop our spiritual practices as we embark on our soul's journey. These practices can be easier for some people than for others. Start small. Try one minute of total solitude. You will find it will go a long way in developing your meditative abilities.

Have patience. This is critical, especially if this concept is new to you. Your soul deserves the very best you have to offer. Why? You *are* your soul. The physical body is merely a rental unit. When you leave your physical body, your soul energy continues. Be patient and kind to yourself. As you work through your meditation and prayer practices, start to feel your soul's tribe that is around you. It can be very subtle at first but trust yourself.

Create a spiritual routine. When we have routines, it grounds us, it helps us to be organized, clears our minds so we can focus on other tasks. We have routines for hygiene– we shower, brush our hair and teeth, do laundry, vacuum. We have routines for finances–we balance our accounts, verify our credit spending, have a savings and investing plan. We have routines for our health–we may have a gym membership, work out at home, or make it a point to go on hikes. So why is it most of us don't have a spiritual plan or routine in place? You may even ask what does a spiritual routine look like?

There are many benefits to communicating with your spiritual team. One of them is to help you stay safe. Have you ever walked into a room, store or even your bedroom and the place felt off or uncomfortable? You can call on your spiritual team to clear the space.

Simply ask your Soul Tribe to remove all dark beings and negative energies that are not for my greater good.

Keep in mind a spiritual law I learned a long time ago. You are only allowed to clear the spaces that you inhabit: your home and property. If you are travelling, it could be a hotel room, car rental or any other space that you would visit. Clearing other people's homes and spaces without their knowledge or permission is a violation. Clearing spaces by removing negative energies and dark entities keeps you spiritually healthy. I also cross over all ghostly souls that come my way. Keep in mind that spiritual jurisdiction is a spiritual law that is designed to balance karma.

Spiritual jurisdiction means that I cannot, without explicit permission from you, clear your home. It is no different than my needing to knock on your door or ring your doorbell and you let me inside. For example, I would never walk into your home and borrow your food processor without asking. Right? The concept is the same, and it is no different in these other dimensions.

Once I had a conversation with a woman who could remote view, and she was telling me she would constantly remote view her married children's homes. That is a gross violation of their privacy, especially since she could remote view in real time, from a distance, and see what her kids were doing in their house.

My basic daily spiritual routine is something like this:

- In the evening, before bed, I remote view my home or hotel space to cross over any ghosts, transmute dark energies, and remove any dark entities.
- I thank my Soul Tribe for their help and guidance for the day.
- I request that my Soul Tribe protect me while I sleep.
- In the mornings, I spend a few minutes in prayer, talking to Source and my Soul Tribe.

- Then I meditate and listen to my Soul Tribe. What messages do they have to tell me?
- Lastly, I set my daily intentions, while asking for wisdom, as I go about my day.

Mediation is a key element as we embark on our spiritual path. It helps to open up that divine pathway by bringing back awareness and balance into our lives. It also helps us to connect to our Soul Tribe and enables us to slow down so we can think clearly. By meditating on a regular basis, you will find that you become more thoughtful in your words, deeds, and actions, because you are now responding from a place of inner knowing and wisdom.

Our free will actions, and choices, are now becoming higher frequency. It helps us to stop and listen to situations as they arise, and not to have a knee jerk reaction. This gives us wisdom and enhances our karmic paths. Mediation will calm us, and it gives us balance as it allows us to listen to that inner voice, a critical part of our Soul Tribe.

Meditation can help us to solve problems, because when we meditate, we allow ourselves a few moments to take a breath and step back. It can also help us to learn how to objectively analyze the lessons we need to learn–from a difficult boss, relatives, friends, co-workers, even a spouse and children.

As we have these human experiences with certain people in our lives, and we take a moment to analyze the situation, we can ask ourselves, "What did I learn from this experience?" This makes the experience richer and deeper, as it gives us a new level of understanding. The meditation doorway also enhances many abilities that I will discuss in a later chapter.

Mediation enhances our intuition because we are listening to our Soul Tribe. And there is a huge bonus: as our intuition increases, so do our psychic abilities, our connections to our Soul Tribe, and to Source. Intuition is our most profound psychic ability. Intuition keeps us safe–when we choose to listen to it.

Intuition is our friend. Intuition lives within

our soul. We own it and we owe it to ourselves to learn how to develop it. We need to utilize this skill to its fullest potential. Why? Because it brings us insight, wisdom and knowledge. The more we trust it, and develop it, the more it connects us to the Divine.

We need to learn to love and embrace our intuition. No one else can do this for us. Many of us have been programmed as children to not believe in ourselves. But, if that is you, you need to know it is never too late. We do not need to wait until we are 70 years old and wish we would have started sooner.

Intuition is one of those skills that most people are inherently born with, but due to most parental programming, it may go dormant within us. This happens when a parent may say something like, "Now that is silly…" or "Stop imagining…." To consciously work on developing your intuition, start small. Maybe you are driving in a location that is not familiar to you. Take a moment, get centered and tell yourself to drive to the appropriate location and see what happens. Remember, developing intuition is a process.

Mediation can start with seemingly mundane levels of insight, and only needs to last a few moments or minutes. As you increase this spiritual practice, your mediations will lengthen and bring you to greater understanding in the wisdom. There is no wrong way to start mediating. You just need to start. Your Soul Tribe will help you if you ask them. As your meditation practices grow, you may find that your sleep cycle improves, along with your health and relationships.

If your spiritual well is empty, meditating can help you to refill it. Mediation is mental nourishment that each of us deserves. If you find you fall asleep while mediating, that is ok. Chances are pretty good that your mediation is continuing and you're listening to your Soul Tribe while you sleep.

Prayer is taking the time to talk to your Soul Tribe and that includes God, Source, Creator, or whatever name you choose to call it. Prayer is focused action. It means that we are seeking advice and help, or giving our gratitude, to Source. If you are in a difficult situation, it's ok to emotionally show that. I have not been shy about complaining about certain circumstances while in prayer to my Soul Tribe and God. I find that it helps with my meditation if I can get things off my chest. ☺

A critical element about prayer. In many religions, we have been taught to pray with our hands closed, folded together. Prayer is a form of energy, and our hands conduct energy. Think about a handshake. When we shake hands with another person, we are feeling that person's energy field. We are, on a subtle level, analyzing that person. Are they trustworthy? Are they kind? Does that person make me want to recoil or go into a defensive mode? Now with prayer, when we pray and close our hands together, we are closing the circuit. That prayer energy does not go out. However, if we pray with open arms, open hands facing up, we are more readily connecting to the higher realms.

Meditation and prayer are gifts that only you can give to yourself. You are worth this time and investment. It may be difficult in the beginning, but as you begin to develop your spiritual practices, it will become easier and more natural for you. Mediation is more passive as we are focused on listening. Prayer is more active as it is our dialogue with our Soul Tribe and Source.

Setting intentions through prayer is your game plan. It is literally the starting point for any dream, desire, or result you wish to achieve. Intentions come from our creative centers. If we can think it and visualize it, then we can intend for it to become reality. Only then can an intention manifest itself into reality. Nothing in this universe happens without intent.

When setting your intentions, make sure you are in a restful and peaceful state of mind, after mediation perhaps, so that you are at your peak when it comes to your mind being cleared of clutter, emotions and any other dramas.

Release any negative thoughts, especially if they center around not feeling worthy. This is a self-destructive programming that many of us arrive with on this planet.

When you set intentions, you are also setting up your personal goals. Some are long-term and some are immediate.

Identifying Your Soul Tribe Members

It's in our human nature to classify everything. It's what helps us stay grounded, give us knowledge, and keep us safe. Why shouldn't this apply to our spiritual world and the other dimensions? Identifying your Soul Tribe is of primary importance.

On the surface, a rattle snake and a garden snake are both snakes. But we, as humans, have different classifications for these snakes for a reason. We have learned they are not the same. A rattlesnake is much different than a garden snake. Think back to a time when you may have gone to the zoo as a child, or even as an adult. If you were to point and say, "Hey, look at that mammal!" What are you talking about? A meerkat? A lion? Peacock? A Komodo dragon? Wait, a Komodo dragon is not a mammal, but you get the idea. Later on in the book, there is a discussion on different types of beings and entities. Knowledge is power, and it is important that we learn to identify our Soul Tribe, making sure there are no impostors or infiltrators.

Why would a dark being, or entity, try to infiltrate your Soul Tribe? The simple answer is because they can. The complicated answer is that these dark beings, who fell from the light of the Divine (Source, Creator…), need an energy source. They need fuel and they can no longer get that energy from the higher realms. As we learned earlier these dark beings learned out that they can use humans as a step-down transformer for their energetic needs. They capitalize on our lower frequency emotions, such as hate and fear. This adds fuel to them. Remember, we have free will and the choices we make affect us and our

Soul Tribe. If they can infiltrate our Soul Tribe, they can then begin to negatively influence us. As this happens, our Soul Tribe will begin to break down, possibly even de-evolving.

How can you ensure your tribe is yours?

Blind trust in any segment of our lives, or soul history, can be dangerous. Performing some due diligence, testing, discernment is what keeps us safe. It ensures we keep our personal power. We constantly use our five human senses to learn about our environment. We see and hear things around us all the time. If something doesn't 'feel' right, our intuition often kicks in to validate what we know. Trust with discernment. Trusting yourself will give you confidence. As you learn to meditate, pray, and develop your intuition, your gut instinct, will grow.

Discernment is critical when it comes to working with the members of your Soul Tribe because there are many nefarious entities out there who seek to destroy your light. They do this for many reasons, but one of the primary reasons is to take your energy as a food or fuel source.

According to Websters, discernment is the quality of being able to grasp and comprehend what is obscure. In a spiritual sense, it is the ability to know, see, or feel with whom, or with what, you are communicating. This concept is the same in all dimensions. In the third dimension, let's say you are a parent and you decide to take your young child to the park. While at the park, there is an ice cream truck. Do you let your four-year-old toddle off to the ice cream truck by themselves, or do you use a level of discernment? No. You walk your child there because of a variety of factors that could negatively impact your child. He could get lost, hit by a car, or even kidnapped. Your discernment as a parent keeps your child safe. Discernment should be used when communicating in all dimensions. Discernment keeps us safe and offers us the opportunity to make wise decisions.

Tools for Discernment and Protection

How can we learn to identify who is in our Soul Tribe? How do you know if they are the good guys or impostors? When you call upon or sense your Soul Tribe is around you, it is important to perform due diligence to ensure they are who you think they are. This helps to keep your soul in a safer space. There are also tools and strategies that are designed to protect you against the unseen forces.

The following is a list of tools and strategies you can use to help you:

- Intuition is one of our most profound psychic abilities. When we learn to utilize and trust our intuition, it keeps us safe. Learning to listen to that quiet, still voice offers us insight and the ability to make wiser decisions.

- Using a pendulum is another way to help access your intuition. It is critical to ensure your pendulum is clean and clear, each and every time you use it, so that your results are not contaminated.

One way to clear your pendulum is to keep it in a small dish of salt. Another is to charge it in pure sunlight. If your pendulum is a crystal, make sure you look up what is appropriate for clearing your pendulum. Some stones don't do well in salt, others don't do well in sunlight. Most are fine in both, but it is important to verify.

- If you feel or sense that you are experiencing negative and dark thoughts, chances are they are not yours. When this happens, take a moment to consciously inhale, pause, and then exhale to push out these thoughts at that instant while saying, "I do not consent. You have no authority over me." When we do this, we consciously break ties to these implanted thoughts. You may have to keep repeating this exercise until the negative thoughts go away. If you continue to experience these negative thoughts that are not your own, try running cold water on your wrists to help break up the thoughts.

- Disconnect your Aka Cords. Our Aka Cords are derived from the concept of the Akashic Records, which were discussed earlier. Our Aka Cords tie us to every person, place, location and thing to which we are connected. If we find we are not feeling well or that something is 'off', and we can't quite put a finger on it, try disconnecting your Aka Cords. Our Aka Cords are connected to our Solar Plexus Chakra area, which sits just below the diaphragm. There are several ways to disconnect the Aka Cords. One simple way is to visualize a selenite knife swooping down to cut the cords. I always disconnect all the cords at once. The good ones always grow back. Here's an important concept: Once you have disconnected your Aka Cords, hand them off to an angel. When you do that, that angel is now connecting your Aka Cords to the higher frequencies of the Angelic Realms. If you need to disconnect your Aka Cords from a narcissist or dark entity, you have now connected them to a much higher frequency and that will be uncomfortable to them. You are not causing harm; you are merely taking your power back.

- Another way is to visualize yourself pouring down a rain of salt all over them. Salt cleanses in all dimensions. It purifies. A negative being, entity or energy cannot handle the frequency of salt. If you visualize yourself pouring salt on your Soul Tribe, and you see, sense, or feel, that all or some of them have left, or shape shifted, count your blessings. This means those beings were not a part of your Soul Tribe and you dodged a bullet.

- You can also visualize yourself pouring Frankincense or Dragon's Blood oils, or resins, over them. These are both very high frequency substances and are very powerful when testing and cleaning up your Soul Tribe.

- Another method of verification is the use of a violet flame. Think about ultraviolet lights and how they are known to kill viruses, bacteria and other pathogens in our physical, third dimensional world. Ultraviolet light is actually a form of the violet flame. Visualize yourself bringing up a violet flame and filling your Soul Tribe with violet flame. You can do salt or violet flame for a few moments, minutes, or as long as you feel like it. Remember, if your Soul Tribe changes or leaves, they were not a part of your team to begin with, and do not feel bad about it.

- Put Frankincense or Myrrh essential oil on your Chakras. This helps to naturally balance and restore them so that you are in better alignment as you connect to your Soul Tribe.

- Visualize and surround yourself inside of a tetrahedron. A tetrahedron is a four-sided pyramid and is geometrically the strongest shape there is. I utilize this shape all the time. I will put myself inside of a tetrahedron while I am out at large events, at a shopping mall, or simply running errands. In the mornings or evenings, I will also visualize my home inside of a tetrahedron and fill it with a violet flame, golden light, the light of Christ Consciousness, or any other high frequency substance to clean and clear my home of dark entities.

- Visualize yourself, your home or even the entire planet enveloped in love, peace and compassion. These are very high frequency emotions that will raise your vibration and the vibration of your Soul Tribe.

- Say or place *The Crossing Over Souls Prayer*, that is found at the end of this book. This prayer helps you to assist souls, that are stuck between dimensions, to cross over and go Home–to the higher realms, to the Heavens. It is very powerful and is one of the most profound forms of spiritual service that we can provide. You can also print copies of this prayer and place them in your purse, cars, and throughout your home. They will act as light portals to help these souls transition Home.

- *The Dark Entity Removal Prayer* is also found at the end of this book. You can use this prayer to clear the dark entities that may come at you. You can also print this prayer, and let it do the work for you by placing it around your home and spaces.

If you feel or sense that you are experiencing negative and dark thoughts, chances are they may not be yours. When this happens, take a moment to consciously inhale, pause and then exhale to push out these thoughts at that instant and say "I do not consent. You have no authority over me." When we do this, we consciously break ties to these implanted thoughts. You may have to keep repeating this exercise.

Do not ask but tell your Soul Tribe to remove all dark entities and energies that are affecting you, immediately. It can be as simple as this statement, "I request that my Soul Tribe remove these dark harasser beings from my space, right now." Keep doing this over and over as needed.

At the same time, we need to be spiritually accountable for our behaviors. Low frequency behaviors can create openings for these dark beings to enter our space. The phrase, "Cleanliness is next to Godliness," has significant meaning. Keeping our bodies, homes, and spaces clean and clear goes a long way towards raising our frequency, so that these dark entities cannot attach to us.

The Fifth Dimension and Above

Beings in the fifth dimension, and above, are the ones we need strive to have in our Soul Tribe. These higher frequency beings are our support team while we are living a mortal life. There are many types of these beings, and they come from many different realms. These beings must, and do, abide by spiritual law. They will not interfere with your free will. This is critical to understand.

They know that we reside in the third dimension and that we are here for the lessons and experiences our souls need while on this mortal journey. The higher realm beings are here to help us, but we must ask them for their help and assistance. This is worth repeating. We have been afforded free will, the ability to make choices, act and react to the environments around us. The beings that reside in the higher dimensions are not allowed to interfere except under certain conditions, such as an emergency situation. Perhaps, you are really tired after a long and stressful day, and you fall asleep while driving behind the wheel. Then all of a sudden, your car swerves and you miss being in an accident when you should have run off the road. It is possible that someone on your Soul Tribe interfered with the collision, because they knew you this would get you off track from whatever timeline you are supposed to be on.

The higher-level beings need for us to ask them for help, assistance, and guidance. They cannot act without it because it's a violation of spiritual law, meaning they would be interfering with your free will. In addition, they can only assist us within the confines of spiritual law. They cannot make another person do something for you or to you. They can't make someone fall in love with you, because that interferes with the other person's free will.

For instance, if you are applying for your dream job, and you ask your Soul Tribe to make sure you get the job over the other applicants, they cannot do that for you. That would mean that they are interfering with the free will of the other applicants and the person doing the hiring. There is a lot of potentially negative karma in that. One thing you could do is to pray for the best possible outcome.

Sometimes these realms are called the heavens, this is where the higher frequency beings reside, including the Angelic Realms, along with other figures such as The Ancients of Days, Lord Babji, Mother Mary, Archangels Michael, Gabriel, Ariel, Raphael, and many others. The Council of Divine Wisdom, Lords of Karma are also in these realms.

When we make requests for help or assistance, we can request they help us with our wisdom and understanding regarding situations in which we find ourselves. We can ask them to help us to carefully craft our words for the best possible outcome. We can request their help to make wise choices.

Every time we reach out to them through our requests, or prayers of gratitude, we connect to them. When we make these connections, it raises our frequency. As we continue to do so, our connections to them become easier and easier. As our abilities to connect to them improve, it is still important to perform due diligence practices to ensure that who they are, is who they are purported to be. Using the list in the Tools of Discernment and Protection, is simply good spiritual practice.

Perhaps the most prolific, in terms of quantity and types of higher realm entities, are those in the Angelic Realms. Everyone has access to angels, so let's learn more about what they are, and how they can help.

Angels

What if we had access to something so precious, so exquisite, a gift from Source that could help us on our spiritual paths while we are living an earthly life? Well, we do. Every one of us has access to angels, the Angelic Realms. Angels are beings of light. They reside from the seventh, and higher realms, or dimensions. The Angelic Realms come from the Divine, from God. These beings do not have free will as we do, but their will is Divine and of service to humans and other mortal creatures. Within the Angelic Realms, there exists politics and hierarchies. Some of the types of angels are the Seraphim, Cherubim,

Archangels, Guardian Angels, and others. The Angelic Realms were created to assist mortal man in many ways. These different types of angels reside in different dimensions, or realms.

Angels are in their own category because there are many types of angels, and they don't all pitch for the same team. There is the concept of fallen angels, those former light beings who fell from the grace of God. This, again, is where discernment is critical for our soul. When calling upon your angels, use the tools and strategies mentioned previously to help ensure you have the good guys.

Humans do not become angels. Angels do not descend from human spirits. They are not leftover human spirits. They are of a different hierarchy and species. Angels descend directly from Source. The idea that Grandma Betty can become your guardian angel is false knowledge, imparted upon us by dark entities, or false angels. A guardian angel will have far greater knowledge and wisdom than even the most advanced of ghostly humans.

Angels are here to serve us, assist us, and help us. Think about these statements for a moment. When your grandma Betty dies, her soul needs to go Home, to the higher realms. When this happens, her soul gets the healing and restoration from the life just lived. She then has access to the Counselors of Divine Wisdom, and other higher-level beings, so she can learn about the life she just lived, and that knowledge becomes a part of her soul.

Angels don't have physical bodies. They are definite and discreet beings. They are of spirit nature and origin. They tend to be invisible, but many people have had visual encounters of them. They intellectually understand mortal life, and they share all of man's emotions and sentiments. There have been many times where I have encountered a ghostly soul, who was tortured and tormented in life so badly, that when I requested an angelic transition team to cross them over, their human story was so tragic, that it made the angels weep because of their profound love for humans, and their want to assist us.

Angels are not a religious dogma, and no single man-made institution can lay sole claim to their existence. How do we know? Every culture throughout the history of our planet has a word or concept for "angel." If they don't exist, then how could this be? The same is true for ghosts and demons.

Angels are our Source. If we allow it, we can have access to all types of angels. They are often found in pairs. They work in teams to best assist us in our needs. What most people don't realize is that we can call upon them at any time. They are messengers from God and are the ones who work closely with humans on earth. They are our bridge between the divine and humanity. Angels are the experts we call on for help in particular situations, but it is only a one-way communication. Angels don't call us, but they will comfort us, be present in all situations we ask, and help us. They will not interfere in our lives unasked.

You can request angels to be present around you and ask for their assistance and guidance. They are here to assist us, and when we can connect to them, we are linking to the higher realms.

There are many types of angels, and we need to call on them for assistance. They cannot help us unless we ask. So, what can we ask our angels to assist us with? Pretty much anything. If you have a child who has difficulty sleeping at night, request a choir of angels to come in and surround him. Are you in a hurry and need a close parking space? Ask your angels to help you find one up close. Are you having difficulty with a sibling? Ask angels to help you with wisdom and understanding. Is your boss being manipulative and narcissistic? Ask angels to accompany you to work. Are you traveling on vacation? Request your car be filled with angels. Are you going to the hospital? Request a trio of angels to stand beside you for the duration of your time there. The list is endless.

Should you save your angelic brownie points for the more important things in life? The quick answer is no. Every time you ask for angelic assistance, you are connecting with your Soul Tribe. You may even be expanding it to add new team members. Why deny your soul that Divine connection? Here is something else that is interesting about angels and the higher realms, they too, earn karma for assisting us. Every time we ask them for help, we connect to Source. Think of the flip side. If you are so concerned about asking too much or don't feel worthy of asking your angels for help, you are denying them an opportunity for karmic growth.

Angels are here to serve humanity. Angels are an important aspect in humanity because they are here to serve, and they are real. They are messengers. They are here to help us mortals. Angels do not have free will like we do. Angels are here to assist us, and only within the confines of spiritual law. What do I mean by confines of spiritual law? An example is that I cannot have an angel make sure I get a job that I want or to make someone love me.

We can request angels to help guide us to make a wise decision. But we can't request that an angel impose on the free will of another person on our behalf. For example, I can't make an angel stop my loved one from being a drug addict.

We have heard of Archangels, Guardian Angels and many other types of angels. If you are new to embarking on this path, I encourage you to reach out to your angels.

When we hear the word angels, we automatically think of Guardian angels and Archangels. These types of angels are not a myth. There is a level of hierarchy to them. They cannot interfere with our free will. Guardian angels are here for just that. They are here to protect us, to the best of their ability, based upon spiritual law. They are not overlords. They cannot control us. They have no desire to control us.

They know we have free will and they have an abiding affection for us. Angels guard us, but do not influence us. For example, if a driver falls asleep at the wheel, they may intervene to keep their human safe. While you must chart your own course, they must make the best possible use of the course you have chosen. They do not intrude into human drama, except in emergencies and usually on the direct order of their superiors. They are the beings that will follow you throughout your whole life and throughout lifetimes.

They are seen throughout the history of our planet, spanning time and cultures. They are, however, karmically earned. Based on human intelligence, spirituality and service to others.

Their appointments are based in accordance of human needs and the Akashic Records we have created throughout our soul's history. Angels can function on both material and spiritual realms. This means they do come from the higher realms down to the third dimension to assist us. They, however, do not live here. They merely assist us.

People can have access to personal angels. These are the angelic forces that we earn. Angels are assigned to us based on spirituality, spiritual service, and soul purposes, or life lessons we need.

Impose on your angels. Many of us have been taught to not ask angels for assistance. We are told that they have better things to do than to help us with our menial problems. Surely angels have better things to do than to help us, right? Wrong. Angels earn karma for helping us. Most of us have been programmed by our parents and institutions that we are not worthy of angelic help. Think about this for a moment. Could this concept stem from the lower realms? The dark entities? Is it possible that they know if we constantly connect to our angels, they lose access to our soul? Yes, that is exactly it. So, start using your angels as often as you can.

You can request angelic help for almost anything. Are you running late for work? Make the request that when you arrive there will be a parking spot open for you. Is your child waking up all night? Ask that angels be in the room with him to comfort him.

If you are new to the concept of utilizing angels on your spiritual path, start with these three basic types of angels. Be creative and enjoy the process of discovering how angels can help you.

Angels of Trust

Call upon your Angels of Trust. They can help you with discernment. Learning how to trust our actions and decisions is pivotal on our mortal journey. Ask these angels to help you to trust yourself, trust your inner wisdom. Trust your decisions. When we begin to learn to trust ourselves, our confidence grows, our frequency increases, and we vibrate at a higher rate. This helps us with connecting to our Soul Tribe. It also helps us to keep our personal power. When we know something, it becomes a part of our essence, our soul. It gives us wisdom, and wisdom enhances our karmic paths because we make better choices.

If you have irrational fears, ask the Angels of Trust to help you release those fears. Ask them to help you understand where the fears from, and literally hand your fears over to them. Angels do not judge us. This is where Angels of Trust fit in to help us.

Angels of Intuition

Intuition is our most powerful psychic ability. Many people have had their intuitive abilities programmed out of them during childhood. Again, these are the dark forces at work. It is up to us to take back our power of intuition. Angels possess powers far beyond human comprehension. For this reason, they can assist us with learning, or relearning, our intuitive abilities.

The beauty of intuition is that we all have the ability to grow and expand it. When we do this, we improve our wisdom, which enables us to raise our frequency. As we raise our frequency, it will more readily connect us to the higher realms.

As we increase our intuitive abilities, our wisdom will grow. Within intuition lies wisdom and intelligence. Intelligence can be a linear construct where the consequences may not be readily apparent. Artificial Intelligence is soul-less construct. It is mechanical and devoid of humanity, and devoid of spirituality. However, it is important because with intelligence we gain knowledge. It can be helpful, but we need the bridge of wisdom to navigate the information. To be wise, or to have wisdom, means that we are able to take our experiences and use intelligence to apply good judgement in a variety of situations. The difference is: Wisdom contains a conscious, spiritual component to it. Intelligence is just the facts.

There are many ways to learn how to tune into and improve intuition. As you develop your intuition, look at it as an experiment or a game. There is no right or wrong. It is simply learning to tap into your higher self. One way to do this is to learn to slow down and to pay attention to details. This practice will enable you to tune in with those around you and get a sense of what someone else may be feeling.

Angels of Sovereignty

We are, first and foremost, spiritual beings. We have incarnated here as human beings, but our soul essence, our spiritual self, is what makes you, you. Sovereignty is a supreme authority over a territory. YOU are your own territory. We need to remember this, especially when it comes to other beings and entities that want to reign control over our soul. This is when negative, destructive, and even soul splitting events can happen. When we lose our soul sovereignty, the Angels of Sovereignty can help us regain it. But we have to remember to ask for help and to be specific in that help.

Angels really love humans and only good can result from our efforts to understand them. They are here for us. They love us unconditionally.

Keep Your Soul Sovereign

As you grow your Soul Tribe, it will help you in many ways. Your soul will also go through many levels of healing. With intention, you can learn to identify and change negative parental programming, and any other conditions which may be holding you back. When you do this, you strengthen your soul's foundation.

The only thing that you truly own is your soul. Your soul's health and well-being are critical for your evolution. When you learn to grow and enhance your Soul Tribe, you are able to raise your frequency, connect to the higher realms, and restore your spiritual DNA.

We all have spiritual teams, whether we are aware of them or not. Our teams change as we grow and evolve. And sometimes de-evolve. It happens. We need to remember that not all teams play for the same side, and there is lot of grey in between.

Our spiritual teams are karmically earned. The spiritual team we start out with at birth changes as we go through life. But the key is simple. I used to be a math teacher and I realize that math is the key. It is about frequency. The more we study, learn, and apply wisdom, the more we are able to raise our frequency. The higher we can raise our frequency, the more we can connect to Source (God, The Divine…).

There are so many nefarious and dark beings out there that want access to your soul. They want to own your soul, and it is up to you to fully realize this and to take your power back. It is time for this spiritual war to be over. It is time to live our lives in love and light. It is time the cabalistic forces are gone and we take back the fourth dimension, and restore it to its proper element. It is time that the fourth dimension become what it once was, a way for us mortals to cross over into the higher realms, the Heavens.

When we can break every soul out of the fourth-dimension matrix, send them home for healing, restoration, and guidance, our souls become sovereign. Our souls continue to live on in love and light. Our souls then rob the dark entities of their feeding frenzy, which they have inflicted upon us. Our soul sovereignty will also help to heal the planet.

Each one of us has a role to play in soul sovereignty. The solution is elegantly simple: We can assist ghostly souls in crossing over upon their mortal death. When we do this, there is no recourse for the fourth dimensional beings to regain access to our souls.

The Crossing Over Souls Prayer

Almighty God,

I respectfully request that you take into your loving arms any and all souls who have found their way to me so that they may go Home to the Heavens, Right Now.

I pray with all my heart that these lost, lonely and cold souls receive the love and compassion they need as they enter the light and warmth of your Divine love, Right Now.

I request that your angelic team wrap these souls in your unconditional love for healing and soul restoration so that they may cross over into the Heavens, Right Now.

I recognize and understand all souls need and deserve to Cross Over to the Heavens, making no judgement of how they lived or died.

I hereby request that your Angelic Team Cross Over these souls to the light bridge into the Heavens, Right Now.

Thank you, God, for your assistance in helping me to help these souls to go Home into Heaven.

In gratitude, Amen.

Dark Entity Removal Prayer

I request a team of arch angels from the higher realms to immediately remove all negative entities and energies that are attached to me in any way, right now.

I request that all forms of black magicians that are influencing my mind, body, and soul be removed from and returned to the proper place, right now.

I hereby break all ties, contracts and vows to all dark entities past, present and future, right now.

I do not consent to these negative beings inhabiting or influencing me now or in the future.

I hereby take back my power from them and request my home and soul be filled with the light, love and protection from the Almighty God Source and cleansed with golden white light, right now.

I request that angels shield me with their

golden white light to protect me.

I request these angels bring healing to me and to my soul tribe, right now.

With love and gratitude, I thank all the Divine beings who have helped clear me.

ABOUT THE AUTHOR

Laura Van Tyne is a remote viewer, speaker, and author.

She specializes in Crossing Over, Parasitic Implant Removal/Etheric Medicine, Quantum Healing Hypnosis, Milab Recovery through Regression Therapy, and Soul Retrieval.

Laura's focus has been the spiritual war and barriers that limit someone from accessing their true potential and experience.

She offers solutions for etheric protection focusing on specific tools and modalities for spiritual protection and raising your frequency to optimize your spiritual health.

For more information, please visit:
www.TheKarmicPath.com